I0157787

FAITHFUL

A Collection of Articles

Doyle Goodspeed

HISPUBLISHING
GROUP

www.hispubg.com | *info@hispubg.com*

HIS Publishing Group
4310 Wiley Post Rd.
Suite 201D
Addison, TX 75001
For information visit www.hispubg.com
Contact publisher at info@hispubg.com

Scripture taken from the King James and The American Standard versions,
which are public domain in the United States.

ISBN-13: 978-0-578-19148-5

Faithful — A Collection of Articles by Doyle Goodspeed
Summary: Weekly spiritual insights by a dedicated man of God. The Word
expressed in a wonderfully challenging way to propel others to greatness—a
perspective directed by the Holy Spirit. — Provided by the publisher.

Printed in the United States of America

Cover illustration by Doyle Goodspeed

10 9 8 7 6 5 4 3 2

CONTENTS

CHURCHES AND HOSPITALS

HAVING SPENT A NUMBER OF YEARS as a Minister of the Word, I have found myself in the hospital many times — mostly in visits intended to encourage people who were sick. The last two weeks my wife and I have both become even better acquainted with those institutions, this time from the other side of the table, as it were. We have been treated well and in both cases our health problems were addressed with skill, hospitality and success. In this time we have come to appreciate the work that people in our hospitals do more than ever before. Near the elevator door and in other positions throughout the facility there are placards posted which identify their names. As I have read these I have been impressed with how similar the work of the hospital and the work of the church are. I think this is only natural since our Leader in the church is called,

The Great Physician. (Matthew 9:12)

He is the One with Whose,

stripes we are healed. (Isaiah 53:5)

In one group of aims this is stated: "Be forthright and truthful in all our actions. Treat all with dignity. Treat everyone as an individual, valuing differences and unique contributions." Would this not make every congregation one that it would be enjoyable to work and worship with? We all would like to be treated this way and for it to work, we have to all treat each other this way.

The next group of aims says: "Take personal responsibility to make things better every day. Get involved. Be creative. Take initiative. Welcome feedback, acknowledge and learn from mistakes and seek improvement. Continually expand knowledge and sharpen skills. Strive to perform reliable and timely service." Imagine a congregation of God's people who tried to live by these rules! Their growth would be rapid. Their influence would be wide-spread. All these points are scriptural. "Expand knowledge" sounds a lot like,

> "*Study to shew yourself approved unto God a workman ...*" (II Timothy. 2:15)

The hospital placard continued under the heading "Teamwork" with these suggestions for their employees: "Listen and communicate openly. Recognize each other for exceptional service. Be positive. Enjoy others. Celebrate successes and share laughter. Welcome ideas and value the concerns of others. Support group planning, problem solving and individual responsibility as a part of a team." As church members we strive to fulfill these aims, not because they are on a hospital's list of suggestions, but because we are members of His body having the same care one for another, and rejoicing or suffering with fellow-members as found in I Corinthians 12.

Doyle Goodspeed

ACCIDENT OR INTELLECTUAL PLAN?

THERE HAVE BEEN TWO REMARKABLE incidents with a significant connection. At the 500th Year Anniversary of the Copernican Theory, an outstanding scientist who had been invited to speak at the celebration said the more research he did the more convinced he became that everything about the earth pointed to it being created for the benefit of man. If you think for a moment about the air we breathe, the food we eat and the things we desire and need and how wonderfully all these are supplied by the world in which we live, it makes sense. It was also said that to think that the world came into existence by chance was as incredible as believing that you could put a ream of paper and a fountain pen in a container and shake them long enough to come out with an epic literary work like Homer's Iliad.

The second thing happened at Baylor University in Waco, Texas. A European scientist was hired by the school to head up a scientific research program. In a speech he reported that he had become convinced that all creatures in the animal kingdom are to fantastically made for their existence to be explained by evolution. These incidents caused much consternation on the part of scientists who were inclined toward atheism and evolution. The European scientist was fired by Baylor for having made his statement. These happenings support something I have regularly observed in the Biblical

Archeology Review: there are some pseudo scientists who reject any evidence that does not harmonize with their cherished notions.

It is not essential to faith to have scientific research bear out the existence of God and the truth of the Bible. Biblical faith comes from the Word of God, Romans 10:17. Such study results in a firm belief that God is and that what He has promised He is able to perform. Another quality of that faith is the strong determination to "let God be true and every man a liar." Given a fair chance, scientific research bolsters the validity and truth of the Bible.

> *"So God created man in His own image, in the image of God created He him; male and female created He them. And God blessed them and said unto them, Be fruitful and multiply, and replenish the earth, and subdue it: and have dominion over the fish of the sea, and over the fowl of the air, and over every living thing that moves upon the earth."*

So says the Bible in Genesis 1:27, 28.

Nothing in science disproves this or any other scripture. Science is defined in Webster's Encyclopedic Unabridged Dictionary as "a branch of knowledge or study dealing with a body of facts or truths." Evolution is still a theory, not fact. Explanations for the existence of the world like the Big Bang Theory are just theories. You don't have to be a naïve dim-wit to believe the Truth of God.

Doyle Goodspeed

HOW CAN ONE KNOW?

WHEN THE CALL CAME HE WAS LOOKING forward to a little time off with his family. But one of those emergencies had arisen that called for his expertise. An address was given him and he was to go to the house indicated. He left, expecting to return soon just as he had many times before in his career as a lawman. A back-up fellow policeman would join him. The woman who answered the door told them the man they were looking for was not there, but they wanted to look through the premises anyway. When he opened a bedroom door, shots were exchanged and he caught a slug in the head. The shot was not immediately fatal. He lingered in the hospital in a coma for a number of hours, then died, never having regained consciousness.

His wife was too stricken to talk to the media for a few days, but finally summoned enough composure to face the cameras. She kept whispering a recurring theme: "I don't think I even kissed him and told him goodbye? How do you know when the last time will be? How can you know?" The thought was almost more than she could bear.

This incident suggests a truth of our human existence. Life is very fragile. There are so many things that can bring the end. Most of us have already experienced hundreds of things that almost did. Yet you and I are still here, while thousands of our contemporaries have departed. How can we know which day will be our last day? How can we know when we say goodbye to a loved one that it will be the last? The only thing we can be sure of is that there will be a last day, there will be a last kiss, there will be a last hug, and a last goodbye. And of this we can be fairly sure: there probably will be no signal or forewarning. The huge lesson is that we need to live each day as if it were our last and treat all those we meet as if it were our last meeting. Christ, in His teaching, did all He could to impress that we also need to live so that when that time comes we will be spiritually prepared.

> *"In such an hour as you think not the Son of Man cometh..."*
> *(Matthew 24:44)*

The parable of the wise virgins who were prepared and had oil enough for their lamps and the foolish ones who were unprepared closes with the thought:

> *"Watch therefore, for you know neither the day nor the hour when the Son of Man cometh." (Matthew 25:13)*

And elsewhere, in speaking of ungodly servants He said,

> *"The lord of that servant shall come in a day when he looketh not for him, and in an hour that he is not aware of." (Matthew 24:50)*

We would do well to treat every day as our last. One of these days it will be!

Doyle Goodspeed

WHEN WHAT IF BECOMES WHAT IS

DR. RANDY PAUSCH WAS SELECTED among top academics in the U.S. to deliver the 2007 lecture for the "Last Lecture" series at Carnegie Mellon University: Each year a top man in the teaching field is selected to suppose that this was to be his last lecture. What would he say? What information that deeply matters to him would he wish to impart? This is really not all that unusual. Most preachers have delivered sermons they called, "If This Were My Last Sermon." However, in the case of Dr. Pausch there was a tragic irony. He prepared and delivered the lecture alright. But before the date came for the delivery, Dr. Pausch was diagnosed with incurable pancreatic cancer and told that he had six months to live! The irony of these facts caught the attention of the world!

The brevity of life, the certainty of death, and the uncertainty of when death will come are subjects that are often dwelt upon in the scriptures. In the last part of l Samuel 15 Agag, the Amalekite King said, "Surely the bitterness of death is past" just instants before Samuel, the prophet and priest, "hewed Agag to pieces before the Lord in Gilgal."

The New Testament writers also convey the same lesson of the brevity of life and the uncertainty of it. Paul said, "Redeem the time because the days are evil" in Ephesians 5:16 to impress upon us the need to take full advantage of every moment and make up for lost time. An in Romans 13:11 he said,

> "...*now it is high time to awake out of our sleep: For now is*
> *our salvation nearer than when we first believed.*"

And the same apostle says in II Corinthians 6:2,

> "*For He (God) saith, I have heard thee in a time accepted, and*
> *in the day of salvation have I accepted thee: behold now is the*
> *accepted time; behold, now is the day of salvation.*"

It is not received very thoughtfully for us to be reminded that every day should be lived as if it were our last. And yet we know that there will be a last day for each of us. A young lady in her early twenties was asked on T.V., "What do you expect to do when you are in your thirties?" She replied, "Why, I don't even think about that!" She was living for the day and even the possibility of death was remote. But she was positive in her own mind that she would still be alive and active. A sixty year old man said, "I figure I've got twenty more good years!" But does he?

The only way to be sure we can stand before God in judgment in an acceptable manner is to try to live each day, and even each moment, as if it were our last. There will come a day when "What if?" becomes "What is." And when that time comes it will be too late to do anything about preparation.

Doyle Goodspeed

HE'S NOT REALLY A GOOD GUY!

SHE HAS A MANNER OF THINKING that keeps the whole family entertained. She's still a couple of years shy of kindergarten age. The other day her mother noticed that she was especially troubled and finally asked her, "What's the matter? Why are you so worried?" The little girl replied, "I just can't keep from having good thoughts about the devil. He just doesn't seem like such a bad guy!" Her mother, in spite of several years of teaching Bible classes and having two older children that she had brought through the difficult question period, struggled to give her a satisfactory answer. It was a serious situation but it was hard not to laugh.

Actually, Olivia had hit upon the crux of the problem. Too often the Devil, in his deceit and persistence in trying to win us to his side, doesn't reveal the difficulties that we will encounter if we follow where his temptations lead us. Adam and Eve learned this the hard way. And we still suffer the consequence of death. The eternal consequence we can escape if we follow Him who caused it to be possible for Death to be swallowed up in victory. I Corinthians 15:54.

In II Corinthians 11:3 Paul said,

> "But I fear, lest by any means, as the serpent beguiled Eve through his subtilty, so your minds should be corrupted from the simplicity that is in Christ."

Verse 14,

"For Satan himself is transformed into an angel of light."

Verse 15,

"Therefore it is no great thing if his ministers also be transformed as the ministers of righteousness; whose end shall be according to their works."

Anyone who has struggled to live a life that is circumspect has become painfully aware that it isn't the course of least resistance. There is always the temptation to do the opposite of what we should do. Or as Paul told the Galatian churches,

"For the flesh lusteth against the Spirit, and the Spirit against the flesh; for these are contrary the one to the other; so that ye may not do the things that ye would" (Chapter 5:17)

Ye may not do the things that ye would!! When we become Christians and begin to try to the best of our ability to live as Christ did we feel the force of this truth. Without the light of God's Word to illuminate how we should live we would be miserable creatures indeed.

Becoming a Christian is described this way in Colossians 1:13,

"Who hath delivered us out of the power of darkness, and hath translated us into the kingdom of His dear Son."

But we need to have the thought always before us: having escaped the power of Satan doesn't end the battle. In writing to Timothy, Paul cautioned, "For some have already turned aside after Satan." When this happens, another Apostle, Peter, describes the awful condition. *"For it were better for them not to have known the way of righteousness, than, after knowing it, to turn back from the holy* commandment delivered unto them. It has happened unto them according to the true proverb, the dog turning to his own vomit, and the sow that had washed to her wallowing in the mire." (II Peter 2:21- 22)

Doyle Goodspeed

FAITHFUL

THE VALUE OF SIMPLICITY

As is often the case, a cartoon children's story emphasized a successful living principle—the power of simplicity. The setting was an expensive and famous cafe. The conflict in the story was the struggle of a lowly kitchen helper to become famous and win the attention of his girlfriend. To become a real chef was his grandest ambition. When his opportunity came, a talented rat got into the kitchen and helped him put together a dish that wowed the critics and the crowd. (That can happen in cartoons!) The kitchen helper became a famous chef with a rat for an assistant and won the hand of the girl and they were set to live happily ever after. The dish that brought all of this to pass was ratatouille, a sort of peasant's stew often made of leftovers. To those of us who grew up on red beans and cornbread, this story makes perfect sense. Simplicity makes a powerful statement.

Willie Mays (or maybe it was Jackie Robinson, both were great players), when asked for the secret of his success as a baseball player, said, "All I know is when they throw it I hit it and when they hit it I catch it." It couldn't be any simpler than that! Vince Lombardi, the famous coach who led the Green Bay Packers, found success with the basics of tackling and running. The Packers usually didn't score high but they won! Lombardi believed in simplicity.

The Apostle, Paul, also believed in simplicity:

> "But I fear, lest by any means, as the serpent beguiled Eve

in his craftiness, your minds should be corrupted from the simplicity and the purity that is toward Christ," (II Corinthians 11:3)

A recent popular news magazine played up what they claimed to be a national trend for people to want to go back to the "High" type of worship such as was used when the masses were said in Latin and the worshipers didn't really understand what was going on. In such worship, how could the scripture telling us to worship in Spirit and Truth be carried out? John 4:24

Church growth is simple: when you teach the gospel of Christ to enough people many will become Christians. Why? Because God said,

> *"...my word that goeth forth out of my mouth shall not return unto me void, but it shall accomplish that which I please and, it shall prosper in the thing whereunto I sent it," (Isaiah 55:11)*

The same principle of simplicity applies to our happiness in living a faithful, Christian life. If we add those things usually called virtues to our faith, God says we will not stumble and our calling and election will be made sure, (II Peter 2:5-11). If we walk by the Spirit and develop the fruit of the Spirit (Galatians 5:16-24) we can live a happy and fulfilled life.

One older, wise preacher used to say the Christian life was simple but not easy. But it is better than the alternative. Proverbs 13:15 says,

> *"Good understanding giveth favor; but the way of the transgressor is hard."*

Doyle Goodspeed

A BRISK TRADE IN SOULS

ADAM BURTLE OF WOODINVILLE, WASHINGTON, did what many do with less fanfare—he sold his soul. He offered it in a listing in an internet auction company's ads. He had underestimated what his soul was worth to anyone else. The bidding started at 5 cents and topped out at $400.00. The auction company removed the listing and suspended Mr. Burtle, a twenty year old, from using the site. The buyer, a woman from Des Moines, Iowa, will have to settle for a night on the town or his natural death, said Mr. Burtle, "Due to the difficulties involved with removing my soul."

This bit of foolishness points up a valuable lesson: one's soul is of small value to anyone else. But life, death, the judgement, and eternal afterlife will vindicate the scriptural claim made by Jesus Himself that the value of one's soul is greatest to the owner, (Mark 8:36).

The world's literature is filled with the idea of selling one's soul—consider The Devil and Daniel Webster, by Stephen Vincent Benet. And there are vague reminders in the oft used phrase of one "selling out."

In the Old Testament, when Elijah, that outspoken, rough mannered prophet who was the model for that equally rough clothed, outspoken New Testament prophet, John the baptiser, found the evil King Ahab to pronounce Ahab's and Jezebel's doom, Ahab asked, in a voice no doubt dripping with sarcasm, "Hast thou found me, 0 mine enemy?" Elisha answered, "I have found thee because thou hast sold thyself to do that which is evil in the sight of Jehovah."

'Thou hast sold thyself!" One of the most despicable blights on humankind is slavery. But one did not sell himself, perhaps with the exception of indentured servants who would sell themselves on a contract for a specified number of years in return for passage to America from Europe. Ahab, knowing God, knowing the requirements of God for right living, knowing that he, Ahab, was in the responsible position of king over God's people, was willing to give up all that he had in exchange for the pleasures of sin for a season. Consider the other side.

> *"Moses chose rather to share ill treatment with the people of God than to enjoy the pleasures of sin for a season; accounting the reproach of Christ greater riches than the treasures of Egypt: for he looked for the recompense of reward." (Hebrews 11:25, 26)*

Selling one's soul is not really that rare. People do it all the time. Only usually it is not recognized for what it is. It occurs any time we give up allegiance and commitment to God in exchange for whatever we let keep us from Him. It happens every day—sometimes for less than $400.00!

Doyle Goodspeed

PROTECT YOUR IDENTITY

IDENTITY IS A MATTER OF MUCH CONCERN these days. In almost any conversation within a group of folks the subject will come up. It has to do with the ability of those with a criminal intent using data to impersonate us so that they can buy things in our stead. We have heard of some even having houses purchased against their credit. More commonly, there will be exorbitant charges made against our credit or credit card, sometimes to the extent that we could hardly ever pay them off—at least within this lifetime. This is bad and truly should be a matter of concern.

But in a real sense, no one can steal our true identity. The dictionary describes identity as "the true character or personality of a person or thing." In that sense no one could steal our identity. We alone can form our identity by the things we believe and do. All our lifetime we are building identity. A Christian builds his identity as he nurtures those qualities taught by Christ. Sadly, in a moment of weakness, an admirable identity can be destroyed.

Jonah, one of the minor prophets, was asked who he was and his explanation of his identity was: "I am a Hebrew; and I fear Jehovah the God of heaven who hath made the sea and the dry land." Very simple! It doesn't say much but it says it all.

A Christian lady who lived behind the Iron Curtain, but managed to come to the U.S. as a refugee with her husband and two little daughters, said, "We worshiped God exactly as Christians worshiped in the New Testament times. Being a Christian was the uppermost thing in our life. We were conscious that, as Christians, we could be arrested at any time and imprisoned."

How would you identify yourself in two sentences? Would you mention first your family? Your occupation? The state where you're from? What you are religiously? Would your first sentence be "I am a Christian, dedicated to God, Christ and His church?" There will be a time when that will be the most important point of identity you could have.

It is interesting that in the case of Jonah, here was a man explaining that he feared Jehovah and yet he was, even at the moment, trying to evade God's command for him to go to Ninevah and preach to the people. He had not told the sailors who he was until the winds arose and the waves threatened to heave them all into the deep.

Too often our identity belies our actions. We are Christians and fear Jehovah and yet fail to put Him first in our lives. It isn't very consistent to say we fear Jehovah and then in our lives fail to follow His orders for how we should live and how we should worship.

Protecting our identity is a pretty big job. It's a day by day, even minute by minute, matter. And as important as it is to protect our financial identity, it's even more important to protect our real character that says who we really are!

Doyle Goodspeed

THE GATEWAY TO KNOWLEDGE

THE GENIUS AND INSPIRATION OF HELEN KELLER could well have never become known. She became blind, dumb and deaf when little more than an infant due to a tragic disease. When the family engaged Anne Sullivan to be her teacher and caretaker she was six and a half years old and had been allowed to run rampant without any discipline. They could not communicate with her. In her temper tantrums she would kick, push and pinch. The tantrums were the result of her frustration at not being able to break from a world of darkness and silence. At the table she would walk around and feel the food of each diner. Her parents did not try to control her. They didn't know how.

Anne Sullivan immediately began a regimen of discipline, some of it physical. When Helen would reach over and put her hand in Miss Sullivan's plate, Miss Sullivan would slap it and push it back to her own plate. When she finally got the proper response, she would write "Good girl!" in the palm of her hand. The father wanted to send the teacher away and it was only through the intervention of Helen's mother that she was able to stay—and that only barely. The father was convinced they could never teach a child who could neither see, hear nor speak. Miss Sullivan insisted that the protesting father leave the room while she worked with the stubborn little girl and as she did so she made this statement: "Obedience is the gateway through which knowledge comes!" Under Anne Sullivan's training Helen Keller learned to read and write and, finally, even to speak. She graduated from Radcliffe College cum laude in 1904 and her fame went throughout the world. From her letters and speeches the undying love she had for her teacher is evident. But it would never have happened if she had not learned that first lesson on obedience and discipline.

We live in a nation today with inconsistent ideas concerning God. On the one hand, there seems to be a wide recognition of His existence. The Passion, the movie that depicted the death of Christ, was widely accepted. National heroes acknowledge the help of God with gratitude. Sports figures thank God for their abilities. Movie stars thank Him for winning awards. Crowds fill Mega-churches. But on the other hand, lifestyles and events are antagonistic to the will of God as He revealed it to us in His Word. Obedience to God seems to be a foreign idea.

The entire Bible stresses the absolute 'need for obedience to God. The Psalmist said,

> "*The fear of the Lord is the beginning of wisdom; a good understanding have all they that do His commandments,*" *(Psalms 111:10)*

And Isaiah, the prophet, taught us, "Come now let us reason together saith the Lord: though your sins be as scarlet, they shall be as white as snow; though they be red like crimson, they shall be as wool. If you be willing and obedient, ye shall eat of the fat of the land. But if you refuse and rebel, you shall be devoured of the sword. The mouth of the Lord hath spoken it." Discipline is important in any aspect of life. It is absolutely essential in our relationship to God if we want to please Him!

Doyle Goodspeed

NEGOTIABLE OR NON-NEGOTIABLE?

OUR MAIL THE OTHER DAY, LIKE EVERYBODY else's I suppose, contained a lot of junk-mail. Most of it was an attempt to sell us something. But one word kept popping up so much that it kind of stuck in my mind. Long after I had finished with the mail I continued to think of the word. It was natural that it stayed with me later in the day as I engaged in Bible Study. Really, it was an expression rather than a single word. Certain things would be mentioned as negotiable or not negotiable. By those terms we understand that some things are priced firmly and other things may be purchased with the best offer tendered.

Considering the comparison between what Christ says he expects of the Christian and what we see Christians doing by way of service and faithfulness, it seems there is the feeling that God can be expected to come down to whatever degree of service we see fit to offer Him. Would that not fit the description of negotiating? Do we not say, "Lord, I know what you require of me, but here is what I am willing to give — this is my best offer!"

In giving to God, we know what He demands but we feel we are doing the tipping and so He should be happy with whatever we decide to give. We know He has said we are not to forsake the assembling of ourselves, but, hey, here's our offer. We know what He says in regard to loving our fellowman, what qualities we are to add to our faith in developing as Christians, and we could go on and on about His expectations, but we have a certain offer we are going to make and that's it.

In II Kings 5 Naaman was told by God's prophet to dip seven times in the River Jordan. Naaman was going to modify God's demand until his servant interceded. It was only then that he was cleansed of his leprosy.

Nadab and Abihu, sons of Aaron who were anointed priests, died because they offered unauthorized fire in administering their office as priests, (Numbers 3).

In I Chronicles 13:7-14 when Uzza reached forth to steady the ark of the covenant when it appeared to be ready to fall he was smitten by God and lost his life. Instructions given by God to Moses regarding the ark were non-negotiable but ignored.

In Matthew 7:21-27 Christ concluded the Sermon on the Mount with teaching that validates all that is involved in this essay by saying,

> *"Not everyone that sayeth unto me Lord, Lord, shall enter into the kingdom of heaven; but he that doeth the will of my father who is in heaven."*

Then Christ gives a powerful picture to reinforce the statement. If you disagree with the thrust of this lesson, turn to that scripture and see if that is not a correct summation of the fact that God's Word is non-negotiable. The magnificence of our Creator demands that we bow to His scepter. Doing so brings wonderful results. Failure to recognize that will result in terrible things that cannot be reversed.

Doyle Goodspeed

URIAH, THE HITTITE

IT HAS A BEAUTIFUL WOMAN, HER ENTICEMENT by a powerful man, adultery, and finally the murder of her husband—things which capture and hold the attention of folks. So much is this true of the Bible story of David and Bathsheba that we forget entirely to realize the integrity of character of Bathsheba's husband, Uriah, the Hittite.

Uriah was one of the top soldiers in David's army. He was a brave and valiant man. When Bathsheba sent word to the king that David's affair with her, an affair forced upon her, had resulted in pregnancy, David sent a message to Commander-in-Chief Joab saying Uriah should be sent to David immediately. When Uriah came, David sought to have him spend the night at home, thinking that such a move would result in Uriah thinking later that the baby was his. Uriah refused to go home saying, "My lord Joab, and the servants of my lord are encamped in the open field, and shall I go to my house and eat and drink and be with my wife? I will not do this thing!" The second night David got Uriah drunk, hoping that his determination would be weakened. Uriah still refused to go to his house.

Uriah's reliability and honesty were so predictable that David sent Uriah's death message back to Joab at the battle front by the victim himself, not fearing that the contents would be opened in some way. The orders to Joab were to place Uriah in the forefront of battle, then draw back from him, assuring that he would be killed. The plan worked. Uriah was killed. Bathsheba mourned the loss of a husband and David rejoiced that his sin would be hidden. With Uriah out of the way, David took Bathsheba as his own wife. The baby died. David repented, when confronted by Nathan, the prophet who spoke that unveiling sentence, "Thou art the man." The union later produced the next king, Solomon.

To the depraved of the world, the story of David and Bathsheba became a beautiful love story. When told from Uriah's viewpoint it is a story of attention forced upon a woman, a terribly wronged husband, deceit, and, finally, murder. Not things we want to see connected with our hero, David the King.

There are things to admire about Uriah. He was a foreigner who had risen to the top in Israel's army. It encourages us to see the strength of this man's conviction. Perhaps, too, it should encourage us to see that, upon repentance, even terrible sins can be forgiven. God forgave David, although he was punished. David never forgave himself. He said in Psalms 51:3,

"I know my transgressions; and my sin is ever before me."

His godly sorrow produced a genuine repentance and his remaining years seemed to be spent in an effort to atone.

Note: The references for this article are found in II Samuel 11-12; II Samuel 23:39; I Chronicles 11:41

Doyle Goodspeed

DRUDGERY OR JOY?

IT IS A MATTER OF CONSTANT AMAZEMENT to me that attitude can have such an important impact on how we feel as we work at a particular job. Take for instance, the matter of picking up nails. While our schoolmates were sentenced to the glory of cotton picking, my brothers and I were given the menial task of picking up nails from our yard when we lived in the country in Wichita County, Texas. It was kind of degrading. I mean our school-mates had a ready-made by-word. Like, "Just a cottin pickin minute!" But whoever heard of, "Just a nail pickin' minute?" I mean, you can see how handicapped we were.

Our house was built on a lot where a "bull wheel" had been dismantled. "Bull wheels" were gigantic wooden flywheels twelve or fifteen feet high, that were laminated from two inch lumber. They were used in drilling rigs in the oil field. Our house was built from lumber salvaged from these bull wheels. As they were taken apart, the used nails were allowed to fall to the ground with the thought that, after the house was built, the area could be plowed under and the nails would be buried. What was overlooked was that every time it rained, hundreds of nails would come to the surface, and inevitably be picked up in the tires of our or our neighbor's cars, to the immense consternation of all. So they were always saying, "We got a cotton pickin' nail in our tire over at the Goodspeeds." Or something like that. Other words may also have been used. We had some creative neighbors.

The three Goodspeed boys (Henry was not yet born) were periodically given a bucket and instructions to pick up nails. The time drug, minutes seemed like days, muscles ached and we thought relief would never come. When it did, the aches left and we vigorously played the rest of the day rolling old used automobile tires down off the cellar to the road a quarter of a mile away, and back to the house, over and over again. Throughout life, until the present time, I have noticed the same dynamic—if it's something you like, the energy level is high, time passes quickly, and you feel good. If it's something you are not excited about, it's a lot like picking up nails.

You have to know this dynamic to understand what the Biblical author James meant when he said,

> "Count it all joy when you fall into diverse temptations."
> (James 1:2)

Temptation is no fun unless you can know that when you resist, it pleases the Creator. So James explains,

> "Blessed (happy) is the man that endureth temptation: for when he is tried, he shall receive the crown of life, which the Lord has promised to them that love Him." (James 1:12)

The beatitudes in the Sermon on the Mount (Matthew 5) are things that bring happiness only through the understanding that they are the right things to do. Worship can be drudgery or joy, it all depends on your attitude and who you're trying to please. If we love God enough, worship and service are rendered with pleasure. If not, it's like picking up nails!

Doyle Goodspeed

THE DEVIL'S WOODEN HORSES

ONE OF THE ANTI-VIRUS DEVICES ON MY computer just flashed a screen telling me that there had been a "Trojan Horse" attempt to penetrate their defenses of my equipment and they had zapped it. The time of the attempted nefarious attack had occurred while I was typing away, blissfully unaware of any evil that some nameless enemy had sought to do me. It is scary to realize that I was not singled out because of any personal animosity—some hacker had probably put out the feelers to thousands of others and many of them, not recognizing the danger to their computer for what it was, became victims. Every day, I am informed of other attempts to infect me with a computer virus. The inventive terms used to notify me are descriptive and clever. Yesterday the anti-virus folks told me there had been a "back door" attempt. The words they used immediately clued me in on the nature of the attempt even without clicking on the "Details" icon.

By their use of the term, "Trojan Horse" I knew that there had been someone with a diabolical inclination who had tried to do damage to as many computers as possible by offering what seemed to be a free, attractive thing as bait. If I had opened them, the damage was done. Scam artists use the tactic every day. So does the devil. The Greeks also knew about this. The myth tells us of the Greek's victory over the city of Troy. They had laid siege to the city for ten years with no success. So they fashioned a gigantic, hollow, wooden horse into which they placed a number of Greek soldiers and rolled it near the gates of the city. Then they appeared to leave. The people in the city of Troy were delighted at the gift. They also were delighted that their enemy was gone. The trouble was that the night they brought the horse within the city, the hidden Greek soldiers slipped out and opened the gates to the Grecian army which had returned!

Paul knew about Satan's use of Trojan horses. To the Corinthian church he said,

> *"But to whom you forgive anything, I forgive also...that no advantage may be gained over us by Satan: for we are not ignorant of his devices."* *(II Corinthians 2:10-11)*

Many in the Corinthian church did not have good feelings toward Paul but he knew he could not afford the luxury of resenting them. That was a gift Satan offered. But he knew the way that worked. Satan had been doing that since he offered Eve the attractive but forbidden fruit. Paul didn't fall for it! He forgave them.

On television, in movies, and all around us the Devil puts out his offers. We need to examine each and remember,

> *"Your adversary the devil, as a roaring lion, walketh about seeking whom he may devour."* *(I Peter 5:8)*

Doyle Goodspeed

NOTHING WALKS ON AIMLESS FEET

A RECENT PUBLICATION THAT COMES TO OUR house had an eye-opening section on spiders that, to me, illustrated the contention: of many present day scientists that life is too complex to be accounted for by evolution. A number of these scientists have astounded, and even antagonized, the scientific world by stating that such complexity can only be accounted for by accepting the fact that there must be a Supreme Intelligence. There were many interesting things about the spider that such a short article as this present one could not go into. But as an example, there was a discussion and there were macro photographs of the spider's use of webs. Some species of spiders form a domed web, some a bowl shaped one, and others a web that is cone shaped. These are because of specialized types of insects they feed on and methods they use to trap them. The article stated there are seven kinds of webs spiders can spin. Each spider has spinnerets in his aft section like rockets on a rocket ship. Each of these is used for a different kind of web—sticky, smooth, thick, or thin. Without plans or tools he is yet a wondrous architect and builder!

I had not realized that insects are indispensable and form five-sixths of all animal life. Insects are adapted to every land and freshwater habitat. Some live in sea-water. And some even live in pools of crude petroleum, where they eat other insects that fall into it. Insects eat our houses, bite our skin, carry diseases and interfere with human life enough to need to be controlled. But they also play an important and indispensable part in the plan of nature. The decay of carrion is accelerated by insects and they help in breaking down hair and feathers. They aid bacteria. They provide dyes, honey, silk, lacquer and pigments. Many insects control other insects and, in general, they illustrate the wisdom of Ecclesiastes 3:1,

> "To everything there is a season, and a time to every purpose under heaven."

A country philosopher I heard in my youth used to quote a saying he had heard or read, "Nothing walks on aimless feet." The Apostle Paul was applying the same principle when he said,

> "Now ye are the body of Christ, and members in particular."
> (I Corinthians 12:27)

Each part of the body has a function without which the body is handicapped.

This all points to the Biblical truth that our Creator wanted us to know: He has a purpose for us. Not just humankind! Us individually! There is something we can do better than any other can. In the body of Christ, the church, if we fail to find and accomplish this purpose we cannot have the approval of our Maker.

The burning question, then, is are we doing what He placed us here to do? Are we fulfilling that purpose?

Doyle Goodspeed

WHAT WOULD YOU DO?

AN EVENT HAPPENED IN FARAWAY AFGHANISTAN that gives us fodder for thought. The stage was set 15 years ago when Abdul Rahman converted from Islam to Christianity. Recently, he sought custody of his children and relatives told authorities of his conversion. If it had not been for the fact that an American stateswoman was visiting Afghanistan, Mr. Rahman would probably have been executed quickly. But as things transpired, he was being threatened with death, the penalty demanded by Islamic law of one who becomes a Christian. The prosecutors were determined to pursue the case to the point of death. They offered him an "out" if he would renounce Christianity and reaffirm his allegiance to Islam. Mr. Rahman refused. As events worked toward a conclusion, U.S. Secretary of State Condoleezza Rice told Afghanistan's Foreign Minister, Abdullah Abdullah, that the U.S. expected Afghanistan to honor principles of freedom we had fought to help them protect when Afghanistan was being threatened. Germany, Italy, and other European countries stepped in and joined the opposition to Mr. Rahman being killed for his religion and finally, it seems that Mr. Rahman is being allowed to seek asylum in another country.

This causes us to think. What would we, you and I, have done if we were faced with a similar situation? Mr. Rahman's case is not really an isolated one. It grabs our attention because we are so inundated in freedoms that to us it just seems to be an unreality that such a thing could happen. Our situation is the exception, not the rule, for Christians. The Bible speaks of it in this way:

> "...*others were tortured, not accepting their deliverance; that they might obtain a better resurrection; And others had trial of cruel mockings and scourgings, yea, moreover, of bonds and imprisonment: they were stoned, they were sawn asunder, were tempted, were slain with the sword: they wandered in sheepskins and goatskins; being destitute, afflicted, tormented; (of whom the world was not worthy:) they wandered in deserts, in mountains, and in dens and caves of the earth. And these all, having obtained a good report through faith, received not the promise: God having provided some better thing for us, that they, without us should not be made perfect.*" (Hebrews 11:35-40)

Read also Revelation 2:10 and 13

In other countries, even today, we see Christians making similar sacrifices for their faith. But our question is: "What would you and I do?" Or, more appropriately, "What have we done?" That answers the first question. Such examples of heroism and steadfast faith, should inspire us all to greater things.

Doyle Goodspeed

IF IT'S NOT IN THIS BOOK,
IT'S NOT IN THE REAL BOOK

DECEIT IS DESCRIBED IN WEBSTER'S Collegiate Dictionary as, "A device used to deceive." Of Christ, the prophet said,

> *"Neither was deceit found in his mouth."* *(Isaiah 53:9)*

The word, or some form of it, is found many times in the Bible, always with a bad connotation. The deceitfulness of sin is spoken of in Hebrews 3:13. Sometimes we deceive ourselves because we lust to do wrong. James speaks of a man deceiving his own heart in James 1:26. Sometimes we are deceived by others. In II Timothy 3:13,

> *"Evil men and imposters shall wax worse and worse, deceiving and being deceived."*

> *"The devil, the old serpent, the dragon, deceives those that dwell on the earth."* *(Revelation 13:14)*

That would be me, and you. And, therefore, there is much need for the oft given admonition,

> *"Be not deceived"* as in *"Be not deceived, God is not mocked: for whatsoever a man soweth, that shall he also reap."* *(Galatians 6:7)*

There is a billboard that is saturating the Metropolitan area of Dallas with the message: "IF IT'S NOT IN THIS BOOK, IT'S NOT IN THE REAL BOOK." It is speaking of the Yellow Pages. But this thought has a lot of application to the religious world today.

Attention is given to just about every source of authority except the Bible today, when the Bible is the only Book that contains the mind of God. It contains warnings throughout its pages against adding to it or subtracting from it. Deuteronomy 4:2 and Revelation 22: 18-19,

> *"Be not deceived"* is a command with an understood subject of *"you."*

In other words, God is commanding us to "be not deceived." If I allow it, there may be another force such as the devil or a fellow human being who is under the influence of the devil who will be an agent in bringing my deception about, but God still convicts me of the sin because there are things I can do to prevent it. If I pray and study carefully and make sure that all I accept and believe is from the mind of God and is authorized within His divine Word, I can avoid the deceitfulness that results in sin. If it's not in His book, it isn't in the real book.

There is a helpful, but puzzling, account in the Old Testament in I Kings 13 of a prophet who went on a mission for the Lord. He was strictly enjoined,

> *"Do not eat bread or drink water in Bethel. And do not return by the way you came."*

In Bethel, an older prophet told him that God also had given him a message and said it would be alright for him to eat and drink before he returned. He believed the old false prophet in spite of God's strict message to him, and was persuaded to go against what God had said. The result was that he lost his life.

The message in this account is clear: we can know exactly what God wants us to do. No one, or no influence, is to be allowed to move us from that course. He has placed His message to us within a book, the Bible, and if our guidance is from any other source it isn't to be accepted.

Doyle Goodspeed

FAITHFUL

FATAL ATTRACTION

ANCIENT PEOPLE, EVEN THOSE WHO HAD not yet had the advantage of hearing the Bible message, were aware of the struggle between right and wrong. They looked for ways to explain this, as well as other mysteries, and their attempts to explain these resulted in mythology. The myths are interesting and often contain a grain of truth.

The sirens were sea nymphs, half bird and half woman, who had the power to charm all who heard them. Mariners who heard them allowed their judgment and caution to be impaired by the beauty of the songs until, too late, they saw the wrecks of ships and the bones of luckless sailors lying on the reefs. Odysseus passed them safely by having his sailors put wax in their ears so they could not hear. Then, he had them lash him to the mast of the ship so he could hear the songs but would not be able to respond to the temptation. The siren's songs were said to entice with the promise of all manner of joys and pleasures while, all the while, you were being led to certain destruction.

We are all aware of the struggle between right and wrong that is constantly going on within us. At the end of life, our destiny will depend on how well we have understood the nature of the struggle and how successfully we have withstood the temptations.

Indeed, Satan does seek our destruction. He uses deception and the false hope of pleasures of the flesh, the eye and the pride of life. While using wax in our ears or lashing ourselves in such a way as to not be able to respond to him will not work, there are ways we can prepare to avoid his snares. Christ used His knowledge of the scriptures in the wilderness to avoid the clutch of the devil. Adam and Eve fell because they did not dwell on the Word of God. Eve said, "God said we would surely die." The devil said, "You shall not surely die." And they believed the devil. Or, at least Eve did. This was a picture of all sin — temptation comes to lure us away from the right. We escape it by doing the Will of God in our lives. What we are and where we ultimately will be is determined by how hard we try and how successful we are.

The Bible gives us many helps. "Watch and pray that you enter not into temptation," Christ said in Matt. 26:41.

> *"Be sober, be vigilant; because your adversary the devil, as a roaring lion, walketh about seeking whom he may devour: Whom resist steadfast in the faith..." (I Peter 5:8-9a)*

A full picture is given in James 1:13-15,

> *"Let no man say when he is tempted, I am tempted of God; for God cannot be tempted with evil, neither tempteth He any man: but every man is tempted, when he is drawn away of his own lust, and enticed. Then when lust hath conceived, it bringeth forth sin: and sin, when it is finished, bringeth forth death."*

It helps a lot to see sin for what it is and where it leads, not to the pleasure and ecstasy promised in the siren song, but, as God tells us in His Word, "The wages of sin is death."

Doyle Goodspeed

WHAT WE SEE IN THE GLASS

ADAM AND EVE LIVED WITHOUT GLASS windows in their dwelling, even though they are nice to have. God had placed glass in the earth's crust, but it was several generations before it was discovered. A few generations passed and Tubalcain came along. He was

> "an instructor of every artificer in brass and iron."
> (Genesis 4:22)

But it would be over three thousand years before sailors cooking with a sea weed fire on a sandy Shore found the silicon in the sand melting into glass. Chemicals in the ash of the seaweed were essential for the process. At first, glass was mainly used in artwork. Soon, more utilitarian uses became common. This was indeed a boon to mankind since 14% of the earth's crust is glass. Today, it is hard to imagine a world without glass windows, glass buildings, glass utensils, technical products encased in glass, and new items like fiber optics. And mirrors!

By the time of the New Testament, Paul could say,

> "For now we see through a glass darkly; but then face to face." (I Corinthians 13:12)

Darkly? Primitive glass was wavy and imperfect. Glass of even a century ago was lacking in the clarity we see today. Some mirrors were made of highly polished metal like bronze. Mirrors usually are an asset, but not always. Marlene Dietrich had only heavily smoked mirrors in her expensive Park Avenue apartment, it was discovered after her death. She didn't want to be reminded of the ravages of age! We look into a mirror to see what adjustments we can make for the better. She knew she could not do away with what she saw. The Word of God reveals imperfections in us and shows us how they can be remedied, but not all are willing to accept the changes indicated. Some will not even look! They don't like what they would see.

James 1:23-25 says,

> *"For if any be a hearer of the word, and not a doer, he is like unto a man beholding his natural face in a glass: for he beholdeth himself, and goeth his way, and straightway forgetteth what manner of man he was. But whoso looketh into the perfect law of liberty, and continueth therein, he being not a forgetful hearer, but a doer of the work, this man shall be blessed in his deed."*

Repentance is the process by which we improve our spiritual appearance. The only way we can tell if anything is good or bad is through God's telling us. The supreme test is, "What does God say?" We improve our appearance only when we follow that. The faithful Christian is the one who constantly looks for ways to improve. And then does it! It is now easy to imagine a day when the earth and all therein is dissolved and melted. But then we'll be too distracted to watch!

Doyle Goodspeed

FOR WANT OF A NAIL...

THE CAUSE OF THE TERRIFYING COLLAPSE of the Mississippi River Bridge in the twin cities of Minneapolis-St. Paul, Minnesota, has not yet been determined but attention has been called to other similar bridge collapses, the failure of which was determined after extensive investigation. The Silver Bridge connecting West Virginia and Ohio plunged into the Ohio River on December 15, 1967. Like the Minneapolis Bridge, it dumped its load of rush hour traffic into the river below. Forty-six people lost their lives. The cause was finally traced to a single small fastener called an eye bar. It had a tiny one tenth inch defect that caused its failure. The stress caused a domino effect of other failures dropping tons and tons of metal, concrete, cars and people into the river.

The Bible constantly warns us against the tendency to discount the importance of small things. In Judges 5:23 the Bible tells us,

> *"Curse ye Meroz, saith the angel of Jehovah. Curse ye bitterly the inhabitants thereof. Because they came not to the help of Jehovah, to the help of Jehovah against the mighty."*

This denunciation was in the victory song of Deborah, the judge. She had led, along with Barak, the army of the Lord against Sisera, an enemy of God's people. The battle had been successful and God's people were freed. But the point was the small village, so small its location is now questionable, had not sent any men to help with the battle.

We do not know what their excuse was. Our guess would be that they felt their help would be so insignificant that it would not matter.

Most of us who are God's people today are in the one talent class, and, like the one in the parable in Matthew 25:14-30, we have a tendency to bury our talent, forgetting the terrible price we will pay for doing so.

The widow in Mark 12:41-44 had the right idea. She had only two mites which make a farthing, about a sixth of a cent. But she gave it proudly and felt it was important since it was all she had, even her living.

We aren't told what happened the next day but we know that God always keeps His promises and he promised to take care of us if we seek first His Kingdom and His righteousness. (Matthew 6:33) So we are sure she had food, clothing and a place to stay. And more important, she had the satisfied feeling she had done her best.

If we emulated the poor widow, the church would grow and prosper. The treasury would have no lack. The pews would be filled and we would constantly be challenged to keep up with problems like where to put the increase of the kingdom. The gospel would be carried to all the community and to all the world. And we would all have a warm feeling deep down that we had done what we could for the One who has done so much for us. Never discount your worth! You are so valuable that Christ gave His life for you. If we give back to Him we are blessed. If not, we are cursed like Meroz.

Doyle Goodspeed

MATTER OF SALVATION

In a recent discussion of Biblical matters one gentleman, as the Lord's Supper was being discussed, said, "Well, that's not a matter of salvation. As far as I'm concerned there's only three or four things that are matters of salvation. One would be baptism and another would be the virgin birth."

It seems to me that one of the things that is leading us far from the teaching of Christ today is the thinking that a portion of the Word of God can be accepted and a portion rejected depending on our own personal likes and dislikes. Did Christ feel that some of the Word of His Father could be dismissed as not important? Remember that He defended Himself before the Devil by quoting a portion of Deuteronomy 8:3,

> "*Man does not live by bread alone but by every word that proceeds out of the mouth of God." (Matthew 4:4)*

The Apostle Paul told the Ephesian elders,

> "*Therefore, I testify to you this day, that I am innocent of the blood of all men. For I did not shrink from declaring unto you the whole counsel of God." (Acts 20:26-27)*

Notice that he did not tell them, "I taught you everything I considered important from the word of God." He taught them all the Word of God. God had already decided what we needed. Christ said in John 17:17,

"Sanctify them in the truth; Your word is truth."

Deciding what is important and what is not important would be like receiving from a client plans for a house and then changing up all the colors, materials, and configurations to fit our own desires and expecting the owner to be happy with the result.

Twice it is said of Noah,

> *"Thus did Noah; according to all that God had commanded him, so did he." (Genesis 6:22 and 7:5)*

Ten other times the same description is given of men of God. The same is true of men today. Selecting what we want and discarding what we don't want is just another way to describe disobedience.

We owe William Tyndale a great debt of gratitude for translating the Bible into English. For this he was strangled and burned. A motivating factor that caused him to do this was a statement he made and which he believed fervently: "The Bible is the path to God." This is just another way of saying what we are told in Psalms 119:105,

> *"Thy word is a lamp to my feet and a light to my path."*

The life of the Christian is a life that has faith in the word of God to be the power unto salvation. The Bible is filled with the accounts of people who were not pleasing to God because they did not follow His Word. And also of faithful men and women, like Noah, who could be described as he was "... all that God commanded him, so did he."

What better epitaph could be better given to one today? Hebrews chapter 11 is filled with the names of men and women who received God's word and, because of their faith in Him and it, lived lives that pleased Him.

Doyle Goodspeed

APOLOGIZING TO GOD

SO FAR, THE TRIP ACROSS TOWN HAD been uneventful. The little boy, three and a half years old and very mature for his age, was attentively taking in the scenery and keeping a running patter of conversation going with his grandmother who was driving. Suddenly, with no signal or warning, a car in the left lane cut across their path and made a right turn, barely missing their front bumper. The grandmother muttered something like, "That was a stupid thing to do!" The little boy looked at her reproachfully and said, "Grandmother, you shouldn't call people stupid." She replied, "You're right. And I didn't call him stupid. I said what he did was stupid." After a few moments, the little boy had another comment. "You should apologize to God." They drove in silence for a few miles. Finally, he looked again toward his grandmother and asked, "Well, did you?"

One of the most misunderstood requirements our God makes of us is repentance. Before baptism can accomplish its purpose, repentance must take place:

> *"Repent ye and be baptized, every one of you in the name of Jesus Christ for the remission of your sins..."* (Acts 2:38)

Repentance must occur before one can be converted from darkness to light:

> *"Repent ye therefore and turn again that your sins may be blotted out..."* (Acts 3:19)

Jesus was being very emphatic when He said,

> *"Unless ye repent ye shall all likewise perish." (Luke 13:3 and 5)*

Being sorry alone is not repentance, but

> *"godly sorrow worketh repentance." (II Cor. 7:10)*

Repentance is not the actual change that must occur in one's life, but it leads to that change. John the Baptist told the multitudes who came to him to be baptized,

> *"Bring forth therefore fruits worthy of repentance..." (Luke 3:8)*

Repentance happens when we have such respect, awe and love for our Creator that we can feel a deep regret for having offended Him by transgressing His will. To be genuine, that must be followed by actually doing as He tells us to do. It is a terrible thing to become so hardened to sin that we cannot be renewed to repentance. God never arrives at a point where He will not forgive. But we can arrive at a point where we cannot repent. And Hebrews 6:1-8 teaches us that when that happens we are crucifying the Son of God afresh and putting Him to an open shame. Throughout the ages, those who have had the approval of God have been those who, like Nehemiah, can freely say, "I and my father's house have sinned, we have dealt very corruptly with thee." Nehemiah1:6-7 He apologized to God.

We all should apologize to God!... But, did we?

Doyle Goodspeed

INTENDING AND DOING

THE REQUEST WAS NOT UNUSUAL FOR the time and place. The time was the pre-middle years of the 20th century. The place was a country home near the Red River in Texas. The mother asked the child, not very old but old enough to have seen her do what she requested many times. "Catch one of those young white Leghorn roosters and wring its neck." He was proud to be asked. It signified a certain degree of maturity, sort of a rite of passage. But nervous, because he had never personally done such a thing before. He caught the unfortunate candidate for dinner and got a firm hold around its neck and began to swing it around and around. Something was wrong! The chicken's head seemed determined to maintain its integrity. When he released it, the chicken ran drunkenly in circles and did not give up the ghost until a second attempt was more successful! It was hard to tell who was the most distressed by this turn of events, the little boy or the chicken, now flopping around like, well, like a chicken with its head cut off. Sometimes there can be an earnest intention that fails until it is put into concrete action.

This seems to have been the case with the church in Corinth as the Apostle, Paul, writes them in II Corinthians 8, 9. He is writing regarding their giving and he says in 8:11,

> "But now complete the doing also; that as there was the
> readiness to will, so there may be the completion also out of
> your ability."

Their intention was good but it needed to be put into action.

He speaks of this as proving them. He says their giving back to God proves the sincerity of their love in 8:8 and in 8:24 the proof of their love. In 9:13 they are told it is

"the proving of you."

When we profess love for God and the sincerity of our faith it remains to be seen how genuine our profession is until we perform the actual doing of those acts that show those things. It is a little like the utterance of James when he says, through inspiration,

"If a brother or sister be naked and in lack of daily food and one of you say unto them, Go in peace, be ye warmed and filled; and yet you give them not the things needful to the body; what does it profit?"

The point we are trying to make is expressed further in verse 12 chapter 8,

"for if the readiness is there, it is acceptable according as a man hath, not according as he hath not."

We often wax eloquent in telling what we would do if certain things were true. For instance, how liberal we would be if we were millionaires. Someone expressed what Paul is saying in a little poem:

It is not what you'd do with a million

If riches should e'er be your lot,

But what you're doing at present

With the dollar and a quarter you've got."

Doyle Goodspeed

ARE YOU QUALIFIED TO PRAY?

MANY PEOPLE, EVEN MOST PEOPLE never think of there being conditions attached to acceptable and accepted prayer. Prayer is something they can do without. But when they need it, they really need it! Prayer is for emergencies. At least, that's the way they think of it. If things get hopeless, pray. Then if everything works out alright, forget about prayer until the next painful and fearsome emergency. To them, the Biblical command in I Thessalonians 5:17 to pray without ceasing is for religious zealots and fanatics. If the bills seem insurmountable and unpayable, pray. If the engine on the jetliner makes a funny noise, pray. If the Doctor frowns and says, "I think we'd better do some more tests", pray. If the marriage is on the rocks, pray. If the child is burning with fever and gasping for another breath, pray. Otherwise, prayer can be put on the shelf and left for a while. It can always be taken down, dusted off and used in the next emergency. It's not as if they're abandoning the whole idea of prayer.

These folks do not realize that the same Bible that tells us of the power of prayer also tells us there are responsibilities that involve the one who prays that must be kept if a prayer is to be acceptable. And also, we must spend time giving thanks to God and praying for the needs of others.

The Bible says,

"*The supplication of a righteous man avails much in its*

working." (James 5:16)

It behooves me to live right if I want to be able to approach the throne of God with valid requests. Also, the Bible teaches that a selfish prayer is not pleasing to God. James said,

> *"You ask and receive not because you ask amiss, that you may consume it on your own lusts." (James 4:3)*

Another dimension is added when we read Proverbs 28:9,

> *"Whosoever turneth away his ear from hearing the law, even his prayer is abomination."*

This is a sobering thought! If I neglect God's law, if I forget Him at all other times, and only think of Him in emergencies, my prayer has a negative result. I can pray that He will help me to have a proper relationship with Him and that He will help me let His will work in my life. But that involves obedience to Him. James 1:6 tells us we must ask in faith. And John 14:13 says we must ask in the name of Christ. Respect for God demands that we keep His word. It is not reasonable to reject His word, then fall on our knees in a time of adversity and ask for His help!

A catchy sign on a church marquee said, "AN OUNCE OF OBEDIENCE IS WORTH A POUND OF PRAYER." Somebody must have been reading their Bible!

Doyle Goodspeed

A QUIET BUT ESSENTIAL QUALITY

SOMETIMES LIZARDS CAN ALMOST BE INHUMAN! As darkness falls they creep out of the flowerbeds and take their positions on the brick wall near the porch light. Sometimes there will be ten or fifteen of them, visible, positioned like soldiers waiting for the enemy. Only this time it's not the enemy but dinner. As the insects come in, attracted by the light, the lizards sit, flattened against the wall, almost invisible, and defying gravity with the sticky cups on their feet that will enable them to even walk upside down across the ceiling. But after they choose their spot there is no more moving. They will sit, not moving a muscle, until an insect is within reach of their long tongue, then …zap!!! …faster than you can see, the tongue flicks out and the bug miraculously disappears! Then they continue their wait until the next prey gets close enough to zap. They can sit motionless for hours through the night. They are growing rapidly and are healthy, so they must be successful. Tomorrow night they'll be back at their post, waiting to be served. The most important weapon in their arsenal is their patience—well, that and their long sticky tongue! Their patience should be the envy of any serious fisherman. And certainly, it should be the envy of any serious Christian. Because patience is one of the most often commanded qualities.

Patience is so important that we are admonished,

"You have need of patience, that after having done the

will of God, you might receive the promise." (Hebrews 10:36)

The successful Christian will,

"bring forth fruit with patience." (Luke 8:15)

In Hebrews 12:1 we are told to,

"run with patience the race that is set before us."

There are more than 40 scriptures in the New Testament that speak of the need for this important characteristic. If we don't have it, we are told to add it to the virtues in II Peter 1:6. And in Romans 15:4 we are told that "we through patience and comfort of the scriptures might have hope."

Not only do we have all the verses that command us to develop this quality, but there are many other scriptures that use the word "longsuffering" which is the same thing. There could be little doubt about the essentiality of patience and longsuffering if we want to go to heaven.

Patience was the quality that helped Job—(and us)—to endure the sufferings he underwent so that he has become the poster figure for patience.

Longsuffering, or patience, is a part of the fruit of the Spirit. Galatians 5:22. And it will be seen to be present in the character of any Biblical character who has the full approval of God. Abraham is known mostly for his faith and obedience. But he waited twenty-five years to receive the promise of a son through whom all the nations would be blessed. That's being pretty patient! Especially since most of us, when we pray for more patience, want God to give it to us right now!

Doyle Goodspeed

ON BEING AN EXAMPLE

MY FRIEND, DON KERN, LOVED TO TELL his young children that someday when he was away from home in a place where nobody knew him he was going to smoke a big black cigar. Each time, it drew the same barrage of protests that their father, their hero, an upright, disciplined preacher, would even think to do such an unexpected thing.

One day Don found himself travelling by train from Mankato, Minnesota, to Dallas. His mission: to hold a gospel meeting at the church where the Goodspeeds were. He mused, if I ever smoke that big black cigar, this would be the place to do it. Of course, he had no such intention. As the train clickety-clacked on its monotonous way, he began to kibitz the card game the young girl seatmate was playing. Soon they became acquainted. He said, "I know Dallas is a big place, but do you happen to know of a Goodspeed family?" The young lady brightly said, "You mean Doyle and Quitta and their girls? Sure, the girls are my best friends." Don said to himself, "Just my luck!"

Not only is there an All Seeing Eye watching over us, there also is a great cloud of human witnesses, observing our every move and judging what they see. There is not, literally, any such thing as a "secret sin." We would all do well to heed the advice given by Paul to the young widows,

> "...Give no occasion to the adversary to speak reproachfully." (I Timothy 5:14)

By our good example we can encourage others and even teach them how to live. We can demonstrate by our lives the kind of faith a Christian should have. As bad examples, we can cause others to lose their souls and can bring reproach upon the name of Him who died for us. It was the same author speaking to Timothy, who said,

> "*Let no man despise thy youth; but be thou an example of the believers in word, in conversation, in love, in spirit, in faith, in purity.*" *(I Timothy 4:12)*

Of Christ it is said,

> "*For hereunto were you called, because Christ also suffered for us, leaving us an example that we should follow in His steps.*" *(I Peter 2:21)*

The song "Where He Leads Me I Will Follow" says well,"...He the great example is a pattern for me."

Our children will be easier taught to live godly lives if we set the example of leading such lives ourselves. Neighbors and friends will more likely respond to the gospel, if they have seen us live it. Fellow church members will be encouraged to do better if they see us doing better. Husbands and wives will be helped in their Christian walk, if they each can be a proper example to the other.

I'm not going to quote the time worn poem that goes something like, "I'd rather see a sermon than to hear one any day, I'd rather one would walk with me than merely point the way" but, come to think of it, it would be very appropriate. The truth it implies is very important to the Christian.

Doyle Goodspeed

SHARING

In the past he had authority and influence as an elder in one of the largest Churches of Christ in the Dallas area. He had the desirable combination of firm unwavering conviction and generous compassion. The church had flourished, people were helped by his counsel, sinners were converted by his unwavering support of the truth. His family also extended his influence. I and my family likewise benefited since we were supported financially in the mission field by the church where he was an elder. He had always been cheerfully optimistic. But now, a pall had fallen. He had retired from his work. His wife of many years had passed and he was living alone in a facility with assisted living.

In the monthly talks we had when I conducted devotionals at the place of his residence there was a recurring theme: "I am so lonely!" He explained over and over in these visits that since their marriage at an early age, the zest of living came from sharing things with his wife. Everything! Good food was better when shared. A beautiful sunset was only good when shared. His work as a Christian was better. The laughs were better and even the sorrows were more bearable when shared. They truly were joint heirs of the grace of life. Now, the sharing was gone, because she was gone! I tried to encourage him as he had encouraged me in the past. I hope I helped a little, but a month later, he would again say, "I am so lonely!" No amount of encouragement would erase the truth: "They two shall be one flesh!" When half of you is gone how can you not miss it?

Paul told the church in Philippi,

> *"After I left Philippi you were the only church that became my partner by giving blessings and receiving them in return." (Philippians 4:15b, C.E.V.)*

The American Standard translation has it, "...no church had fellowship with me ..." and Webster's Encyclopedic Unabridged Dictionary gives as a definition for fellowship "communion." The King James says, "Communicated with me..." A common definition to all these terms is "shared." As a matter of fact, the dictionary cited above gives sharing as a definition of communing. The Philippian church shared with Paul and Paul shared with them. In chapter 1, verse 5 Paul thanks God for the Philippian church having,

> *"fellowship in furtherance of the gospel."*

They shared with Paul in his evangelism by giving moral and financial help while he engaged in his labors. And since there is no way to avoid the implication in the question "How shall they preach except they be sent?" their work was as important as his. An important, but often overlooked, Christian duty is sharing in the spread of the gospel. If we share in the spread of the gospel, we can also share in the fulfillment of the Great Commission as souls are brought to Christ by that preaching.

There are many encouraging examples of churches today that share in the furtherance of the gospel. Thank God for them! These churches experience a joy beyond expression. Sadly, there are many other examples of churches that are selfish in the use of their Lord's money and spend it all on themselves, neglecting the commission of Christ to "Go therefore and teach all nations."

In spiritual matters we often are both the victim and the perpetrator. Nathaniel Hawthorne says of the preacher who had committed adultery in The Scarlet Letter, "He cheated himself by confessing his sins in general terms." Are we not cheating ourselves of the joy of sharing in the furtherance of the gospel when we fail to recognize the importance of our responsibility under the great commission? And, if I understand at all what the Bible teaches, we also cheat ourselves of a home in glory!

Doyle Goodspeed

FAITHFUL

NAMING RIGHTS

IT WAS INEVITABLE! SOONER OR LATER it had to happen. What with everything from sports arenas to racing teams selling naming rights to their property. The area rodeos are produced in Stetson Arena and American Airlines Sports Complex has games and concerts. Francis Schroeder and Jason Black were expecting and, since they needed a little extra cash, decided to offer for bids the naming rights to their offspring via the Internet. The minimum bid that would be considered is $500,000.00 and as of this writing there have been no bids accepted. Lucky child! Unlucky to have such foolish parents! But lucky that no one has been willing to go along with such foolishness.

It is interesting to me that in Spanish, "Como se llama?", loosely meaning "What's your name" literally means "What are you called?" It would be embarrassing to have to answer to "Alpo." Imagine the sniggers at roll call in elementary school!

But in a sensible and more serious vein, as Christians we have a very sobering responsibility because of the name we wear. It is recorded in Acts 11:26 that,

> *"the disciples were called Christians first at Antioch."*

Through Amos, the Old Testament prophet, God had said

> *"...that the residue of men may seek after the Lord, and all the Gentiles upon whom my name is called." (Amos 9:11-12)*

In rebuking early Christians for showing respect of persons to the rich and lack of respect for the poor, James said,

> "*Do not the rich oppress you, and drag you before the judgement seat? Do not they blaspheme that honorable name by which you are called?*" *(James 2:6-7)*

The Christian wears a name that is above every name and his conduct and speech should reflect the glory of that name.

There are huge benefits attached to confessing the name of Christ before men. Christ said of the one who does,

> "*Him will I confess before my Father who is in heaven.*" *(Matthew 10:32)*

Sometimes there are indignities that must be endured because we are called by His name.

> "*If a man suffer as a Christian, let him not be ashamed but glorify God is this name.*" *(I Peter 4:16)*

Colossians 2, verses 10 and 11 give us an important picture of a coming event that all will experience:

> "*...at the name of Jesus every knee will bow...and every tongue will confess to the glory of God.*"

Revelation 22:4 says that the occupants of heaven will have His name on their foreheads. But you don't have to look there in this life. Just look at the way they live!

Doyle Goodspeed

AN ORDINARY DAY?

It was a day like any other day. The cool breeze from the Tyrrhenian Sea made it pleasant. True, there had been rumbles from the mountain the day before and some of his neighbors had panicked and left the city. But Vesuvius had not really erupted since the eighth century and this was August 24, D. 79. His father had lived here in Pompeii—and his father's father and his father. They were comfortable with the mountain and with such a legacy he was not at all uneasy. He cheerfully went about his household chores—a little proud of his bravery. At noon there was a mighty explosion! It was too late to run now! A river of lava, ash and rock descended on the city. Noxious gases stifled him. Before it was over, 23 feet of lava and debris covered him and the city. It was 2000 years before his body was found. It was encased in lava and ash and had the appearance of a plaster of Paris statue. He had company. Five thousand other citizens of the city who had failed to heed the warnings also perished in the eruption.

Many of the world's most tragic occurrences have been accompanied by warnings. Six to eight thousand people died in the Galveston Hurricane and flood on September 8, 1900 in spite of government warnings to flee the island. A lack of respect for danger seems to be a failing that we as humans need to guard against.

The Bible is filled with such warnings. The Lord, Himself, said,

"Watch therefore: for you know not what hour your Lord

will come. But know this, that if the good man of the house had known in what watch the thief would come, he would have watched and not suffered his house to be broken into. Therefore be also ready; for in an hour that you think not the Son of Man will come." (Matthew 24:42-44)

The description in Revelation 6:12-17 is typical of the Bible pictures of the last day,

"...there was a great earthquake; and the sun became black as sackcloth of hair, and the moon became as blood. The stars of the heaven fell to the earth as a fig tree casts her unripe figs when she is shaken of a great wind. And the heaven departed as a scroll when it is rolled up; and every mountain and island were moved out of their places. The kings of the earth, and the great men, and the rich men and the chief captains, and the mighty men, and every bond man and every free man, hid themselves in the rocks and mountains and said to the mountains and rocks, Fall on us and hide us from the face of Him that sits on the throne, and from the wrath of the Lamb. For the great day of His wrath is come: and who shall be able to stand?"

Pliny the Younger was an eyewitness to the awful destruction of Pompeii from across the Bay of Naples. We all will witness this last day. Mercifully, we have been warned and told how to prepare!

Doyle Goodspeed

OBEDIENCE AND THE WORD

TO SOME OF US, OUR LIVES COULD be divided into segments named after the dogs we had. In mine there were the years I had a cocker spaniel, a water spaniel, a hard headed Irish Setter and another hunting dog whose name I have tried hard to forget. He was the one who, when I fired a gun, would streak for the pickup and hide underneath it. Floppsy, was the beagle who almost killed one of our game chickens. After we disciplined her, we came home one day and the hen had tried to get into the dog house again. Floppsy had, in desperation, held her down under her front paws, unharmed, until we came home. But usually, Floppsy tested the limits. When in the house, she would put one paw on the couch. If nothing happened she would try her nose. Then another paw. And finally all her body. Brutus, a Malamute, was the dog that tried the hardest to please us. His life was totally motivated by a strong desire to make the Goodspeed family happy. He knew he was to stay outside. (You don't share a house with a dog the size of a small horse!) My son and I had gone into town to get a car part and, negligently, left the patio door open. When we returned, Brutus was lying on the patio with his nose precisely on the point on the patio door frame where his nose was out but almost in the room. His soft, brown eyes mirrored a deep longing to go inside, but he never moved beyond the limit. He applied II John 9 in dog fashion and thought that if he did not abide in our teaching he had committed a terrible sin. If Brutus had been human, he would have made a good Christian, obedient to his Master. God's Word teaches we should all have that quality but, sadly, not all have it.

In the Old Testament, King Ahab did not. He was a king over the Northern Kingdom and strongly influenced by sins his wife, Jezebelle, had imported. He persuaded Jehoshaphat, king of the Southern Kingdom, to go with him against Syria and retake Ramoth in Giliad. His four hundred false prophets told him:

> *"Go up; for the Lord will deliver it into thy hands."*
> *Jehoshaphat, being more godly than Ahab, asked if there*
> *were not a prophet of God they could ask. Ahab said,*
> *"There is yet one man, Micaiah, the son of Imlah, but I*
> *hate him because he does not prophesy good concerning*
> *me." (I Kings 22:8)*

Micaiah did prophesy that if Ahab went into battle, he would die. Ahab went against the advice of God, and, as divinely predicted, he was slain in battle. Ahab was determined to have his own way. He gave his life proving that we must obey God. Contrast Ahab's attitude with that of the great prophet and priest, Samuel, who, when only a child, was called by God. His response was,

> *"Speak, Lord, for thy servant heareth." (I Samuel 3:10)*

"Speak Lord; your servant hears!" What a wonderful attitude for one who seeks a heavenly home with the Father. And how diligently should we cultivate an obedience that is cheerful, being happy because we make Him happy. Only in this way can we fulfill our purpose and His!

Doyle Goodspeed

INTERESTING—AND A
LITTLE SURPRISING!

IT WOULD BE INTERESTING TO KNOW what motivates some of the polls that are taken. A book entitled "The Top Ten of Everything" gives the result of polls taken that give information presented as the title indicates. Among other questions, the poll asked for things that produced a morbid and unreasonable fear. Fear of spiders (arachnophobia) topped the list, followed by fear of people and some social situations (anthropophobia); flying (aerophobia); open spaces (agoraphobia); confined spaces (claustrophobia); heights (acrophobia); vomiting (emetophobia); cancer (carcinophobia); thunderstorms (brontophobia); and death (necrophobia). A number of other fears came close. For instance, fear of snakes.

What is interesting, and perhaps revealing, is that not a single person mentioned fear of being eternally lost. And yet, another poll indicated that over 70 percent of the people in America believe in hell. The same number believed in the devil.

In the Bible, the Apostle Paul preached to Felix, the Roman governor, concerning faith in Christ. Paul's sermon had three divisions: righteousness, self-control and the judgement to come. The profligate Felix was deeply touched by the sermon—as would be most people today if we still preached on those things! We seem to be drifting from topics that make people feel uncomfortable. The effect of the sermon was that Felix trembled. An exact translation would be,

> "*Felix, being terrified, answered, 'Go for the present, and when I find an opportunity I will call for you!'*" *(Acts 24:25)*

Since "phobia" is defined as "a morbid and unreasonable fear,"I do not think that fear on the part of one who does not even intend to live according to God's will would qualify. Surely it is not unreasonable to fear a place where there is eternal torment, where the worm dies not and the fire is not quenched. Even as mature a Christian as Paul said,

> "*Knowing therefore the terror of the Lord, we persuade men,*"

And this was right after he had said,

> "*For we must all appear before the judgement seat of Christ; that everyone may receive the things done in the body, according as he has done, whether it is good or bad.*" *(II Corinthians 5:10-11)*

The Biblical pictures of the judgement day depict a serious, solemn, awe-inspiring occasion on which kings, great men, rich men, chief captains, mighty men, bondmen and free will say to the rocks and mountains

> "*Fall on us and hide us from the face of Him that sits on the throne, and from the wrath of the Lamb; for the great day of His wrath is come...*" *(Revelation 6:15-16)*

It would be morbid, unreasonable and unrealistic not to be apprehensive!

Doyle Goodspeed

A TRIAL WITHOUT ERRORS

WHAT WOULD BE YOUR FEELINGS if you were accused of a murder you did not commit but were convicted anyway because false testimony was believed and true facts that would have exonerated you were deliberately withheld? And, then if you spent 27 years in prison for this crime you did not commit?

Of the seventeen men from Dallas County who have been released because of overturned convictions in the last seven years, James Woodard had served the longest — 27 years. A web of errors had resulted in his conviction. One error had been the false testimony of a witness who admitted as much at a later time. But by then, Woodard had spent over a quarter century in jail. It was only when his case was reinvestigated that the truth came to light and it was possible for him to be freed. It was a real case of the "truth shall make you free." The sad thing is that it took 27 years for the truth to be revealed. That's a long time to suffer for someone else's mistake.

No matter how good or bad one's life has been, there is a trial that awaits each one of us that will be the most sobering thing that happens to us in all our existence. The Bible teaches that there will come a time when all humanity will stand before a great white throne to be judged according to what they have done in this life. There will be utter pandemonium as the dead, small and great, are summoned and call for the rocks and mountains to fall on them and hide them from the face of the One on the throne.

But the Bible tells us "the earth and heaven fled away, and there was found no place for them." There was no place to hide. In such a setting each one will be judged. The books will be opened and another book, which is the Book of Life, will also be opened. Then our judgment will begin based upon the things which are written in the books. All we have ever said, thought or done will be brought for the proceeding.

Is it comforting to realize no mistakes will be made? That depends on what the books containing the things we have done reveal. Have we tried to live obedient, righteous lives? We have all made mistakes and God in His mercy has made some allowances. His mercy will soften the blow. And the blood of His Son has the power to do away with those sins we have brought to God to be forgiven. As aliens outside Christ this happens when we obey the Gospel. As Christians who have stumbled, the sins are erased by confession, repentance and prayer. But only those who have lived according to His Will, will come through the trial with a happy result. See Revelation 20:11-15; Revelation 6:12-17; Romans 1:16.17; Matthew 25:31-46; Matthew 7:21; Acts 2:37-38.

A successful trial always needs a careful preparation by the defendant. There's only one time to do the preparation. That time is now, in this life, with God's word the Bible as our only guide. How is your preparation coming along? It's not a light matter!

Doyle Goodspeed

CEMETERY MEDITATIONS

SOMETIMES ONE'S BEST THINKING CAN BE done at the cemetery where dates of births and deaths call attention to the shortness of life and the inevitability of death. Arithmetic is important in the cemetery. It tells you some lived only a few days but none lived very long considering the overall scheme of things. It also reminds you that too much has already been subtracted from what you might expect to be your allotted time.

At this particular cemetery, there were uncomfortable thoughts. In the nearby community, the only public building still standing, the Community Center, sagged on one end and small trees were growing through the porch and all around so that you had to look twice even to see the building. New brick houses on the road had replaced many of the older, early-1900's houses. Talk under the tent that had been set up for "Decoration Day" went back to the era when people killed hogs, canned their own fruits and vegetables, and produced most of what they used. Friends (?) remind you of bygone days when you were taller and thinner and had much more hair! But there are also thoughts of warmly remembered associations with some who have passed on.

Requests to help you locate barely recalled places in the area were met with instructions like, "Go down to where the old cotton gin used to be and turn left." Only, the cotton gin is long gone and a housing development is there now and 20 years have erased the recollection of where the old cotton gin stood!

The words of a song kept traveling through my thoughts: "Change and decay in all around I see. Oh Thou who changest not abide with me."

When we are reminded of the volatility of everything around us, the unchangeable nature of God and His Word becomes even more precious. In Hebrews 6:18,19 the Holy Spirit tells us,

> "By two immutable things, in which it is impossible for God to lie, we might have strong consolation, who have fled for refuge to lay hold on the hope set before us: which hope we have as an anchor of the soul..."

God made promises to us. And God cannot lie. Anchors are as important at the cemetery as they are in a boisterous sea!

Amid great change, the unchangeableness of God and His Word are important because there are some other things that don't change. We still have diseases we can't cure or control, lives and homes that are broken by sin, our own personal struggle with sin, injustices of man to man, children that are abused, and poverty that devastates entire nations. And then, too, there's that other thing—one's own approaching death! A walk through the cemetery reminds us of this.

Doyle Goodspeed

BRING UP A CHILD

THE MOTHER THOUGHT SHE WAS DOING the right thing by her little son as he watched her light up a cigarette and slowly release the smoke out her nostrils. But she said, "Promise Mommy you'll never pick up a cigarette." The little boy startled her with his reply, "Promise me you'll quit." According to her testimonial on the T.V. ad this started her on a successful attempt to put an end to her decade's long habit.

As parents, we often fail to realize the importance of our example. The importance spills over into every aspect of life. The apostle Paul, emphasized this when he said,

> "Be ye imitators of me, even as I also am of Christ." (1 Corinthians 11:1)

The most powerful and effective teaching you and I can do is through a good example. Christ tried to emphasize this while He was on the earth showing us how we could best serve...how else? By His own example. In John 13:12-15,

> "So when He had washed their feet, and taken his garments, and sat down again, he said unto them, know ye what I have done unto you? Ye call me, Teacher, and, Lord, and ye say well; for so I am. If I then the Lord and the Teacher have washed your feet, ye also should wash one another's feet. For I have given you an example, that you

also should do as I have done unto you."

His example of service to us, should powerfully move us to serve each other. There is not a better way to spread His influence than through living His teaching.

Parents are badly mistaken if they feel they can use the "do as I say not as I do" principle in bringing up their children in the nurture and admonition of the Lord as we are commanded to do in Ephesians 6:4. It seems that the phrase that puzzles many in this context when Paul says to fathers "provoke not your children to wrath" is connected to the matter of example. When a father insists on children following a manner of living that he, himself, is unwilling to follow, it will always produce anger and resentment. When young people go through a certain age, they usually look for things in the life of the parent that can be criticized. They have a legitimate excuse if the parent tries to force things upon them that are not shown by their own example.

In II Corinthians 13:5 we are told,

> *"Try your own selves, whether ye are in the faith; prove your own selves."*

This is a matter that gives ample opportunity to test ourselves. Are we really living a life that is fruitful in example? What kind of children will we rear if they follow our example? And if our neighbors are looking for examples of how to live can they see those in us? Would they desire to be what we are religiously? And if they become Christians, would our example cause them to be faithful in moral living and dedication and commitment? If not, that calls for a change in our own lives!

Doyle Goodspeed

THE BEST MAN

I ATTENDED A MEETING MAINLY OF PREACHERS. Most were men with sharp and huge intellectual prowess but physically with much snow on the roof and a tow sack full of aches and pains in the basement. As is usually true of men with such qualities, there was reminiscing. Some of what we remembered even really happened!

One man recalled my association at the first congregation I served as minister with his uncle. As I thought of the man, one who was unselfish and went about doing good, consumed with zeal for Christ, a flood of emotions washed over me. Under the press of the moment I said, "He was the best man I have ever known." I have said the same thing to others about the man— usually under the same circumstance.

Before the meeting dispersed, another minister was speaking of a man with whom we both had ministered. Again, as I thought of that man's devotion to doing right, his dedication to Christ, and his love for humanity, I blurted, "He was the best man I have ever known."

A few days prior, a member of the congregation I now serve spoke of his desire to emulate a former member, one who had moved to Florida, and is now deceased.

When I thought of him, his rare love for people, his sacrificial service, his affection for family and church, his untiring labor for the cause of Christ, I said, "He was the best man I have ever known."

In meditative hours of the night, which are common to those of us with snow on the roof and aches and pains in the basement, I was struck by the thought, "There is something that's not right about this!" Even someone that doesn't know adenoid from adverbs knows that "best" is the superlative. If a thing is best, that's it. Even someone who doesn't know what a tow sack is, knows that! This presents a problem.

One part of the solution, of course, is that I need to amend my ways and make a strong effort to say, "He is one of the best people I've known." The other part is that we know there is only One who is best. That's the One who would have said, "Don't call me best. There is one best — the Father."

I have no doubts about this. The prophet said,

> "*He has borne our griefs and carried our sorrows...he was wounded for our sins...bruised for our iniquities...Jehovah has laid on him the sins of us all.*" *(Isaiah 53:4-6)*

The best people I know, or have known, are best because they imitate Him.

I can make this adjustment, but I'll have to work on it. One is best. The others are very good, but comparatively, they are "some of the best."

Doyle Goodspeed

HAVING A FORM OF GODLINESS

AN EXPERIMENT REMINISCENT OF THE TEMPTATION in the Garden of Eden yielded astonishing results. Reader's Digest placed wallets with identification and $50.00 in local money around the world to see how many would be returned. The wallets were placed on sidewalks, in phone booths, in front of office buildings, discount stores, and churches, in parking lots and restaurants. On one hand some heartening examples were seen. On the other, some disturbing patterns resulted.

A little Asian girl found one wallet in an amusement park in Seattle. Her father told her "You must take this to someone who can help find the owner." They took it to the park office where the father said, "Honesty is the most important thing a child can learn."

A Russian governess found one in a pharmacy and said, "Several years ago I would have taken it, but now I am completely changed. As they say, 'Thou shalt not covet anything that is thy neighbors.'"

People that appeared to be affluent sometimes took the money and ran. People in need often returned it. Brian was out of work and searching for bottles and cans to recycle when he found a wallet in a phone booth and returned it. He expressed the thought that the owner might need the money more than he. A Muslim immediately returned a wallet saying, "I am aware of temptation and how to overcome it." A Buddhist returned one and said, "It is my duty to do good work." In Norway and Denmark every single wallet was returned! The U.S. was way down the list with 67% returned.

The point I would like to make is that people that know better don't always do better. With all the Bibles readily available in the U.S., with all the preaching and teaching, with the emphasis on ethical conduct, I am saddened that our behavior is not consistent with our teaching. One of the marks of the last days was that people would hold,

> "*a form of godliness but deny the power thereof.*" (II Timothy 3:5)

One of the chief targets in the teaching of the Holy Spirit in the book of James was the inconsistency between what we receive from God's Word and how we behave. In verse 22 of chapter I we read,

> "*But be ye doers of the word, and not hearers only, deluding your own selves.*"

This principle is important in all aspects of our lives. Even in the church, some basic Christian principles are held in careless esteem. Dishonesty sometimes goes to church! And yet, honesty is a fruit of the Spirit. Dishonesty is a lust of the flesh.

Honesty, like all Christian virtues, can predominate only when parents teach it and exemplify it. In Norway and Denmark, do they even lock their doors? I remember a day when we didn't in the U.S. Now even a locked door is not sufficient!

Doyle Goodspeed

ABSENT MINDEDNESS CAN HAVE ETERNAL RESULT!

I HAD JUST FINISHED A FUNERAL SERVICE, walked to the car with my Bible in my hand, and opened my car door. Before I could get inside, a member of the family of the deceased called to me. I placed the Bible on the roof of the car and leaving the door ajar engaged in pleasantries with her for a moment then got into my car and drove off. About a block away, a driver behind me began to insistently blow his horn. I thought, "How rude!" until I saw that he was also insistently pointing to the car top. Then "How rude?" became "How nice!" when I realized he was pointing to my Bible, still there on the car top, and unruffled because it was placed so that the air flow hit it just right. I felt very grateful, but also very foolish until a few days later, I read of a woman in the newspaper whose memory lapse eclipsed mine.

A woman in Tinley Park, Illinois, with two small children already in the car, stopped to pick up two more. To make room, she temporarily placed her 2 month old son in a car seat atop the car. In all the confusion and chaos of getting the others seated, she drove off, leaving the baby on the roof. As she went through a busy intersection, the car seat and baby bounced onto the highway and the woman continued on her way. A trucker, a few moments behind her, saw the bundle and stopped. The baby was uninjured except for a few cuts and bruises!

Just before Israel left Egypt, the Passover Feast was instituted with symbolism that was to remind them of the wonderful deliverance God had wrought. When they crossed the Jordan, God had the priests to pick up twelve stones that were stacked as a memorial to remind them of God's power and mercy. With a sharper memory, faithfulness was enhanced.

The Lord's Supper is a weekly memorial of the death of Christ and all it means to us. Paul quotes our Lord as having said, as He instituted it, "This do in remembrance of me." The fresher in our minds the death of Christ is, the greater will be our thanks for it. The sharper our memory of His suffering, the more joyful our submission to Him. Read I Corinthians 11:23-34 for a reminder of the great importance of this Memorial Feast.

How could anyone forget? It happens! The apostle, Peter, says that the Christian that does not add the virtues to his faith,

> "...has forgotten that he was cleansed from his old sins."
> (II Peter 1:9)

And in the same book, chapter 2 and verse 1b, he continues to say that there are those who,

> "...deny even the Master that bought them."

Too many Christians define memory as did the little preschooler, "I think it's what you forget with." Forgetting some things can be fatal — eternally!

Doyle Goodspeed

A DANGEROUS SITUATION

THE NATION WAS SHAKING OFF A DEPRESSION so severe that it is now called, "The Great Depression" and our family, like many others, was hard hit. We were the blessed ones—our father had a job in the northwest Texas oil fields. Low paying, but it was a job. We lived in a tarpaper shack with linoleum floors and calcimined beaverboard walls. Seeing a picture of the setting today, "poverty" would come to mind. But we were happy as we went through the seasons—the spinning-the-top season, the shooting-marbles season, the kite-flying season, the rubber-gun-shooting season, the stilt-walking season, the rolling-old discarded-automobile-tires season along with many others. Our family was stable. The worries of our parents did not seep through to us. The breezes blew and the bright sun shone and life was as idyllic as it could have been in a mansion in the big city—that would have been Burkburnet, population maybe a thousand, a few miles away.

We moved to the REALLY big city, Dallas, when I was eleven and it was a few years before I went back. The first thing I noticed was the huge, overpowering, nauseating, almost lose-your-breakfast type stench of oil and refineries! It dawned on me! "It was there all along! I was just used to it!"

In I Timothy 4:1-2 the Holy Spirit tells us,

> "*But the Spirit says expressly, that in later times some shall*

fall away from the faith, giving heed to seducing spirits and doctrines of demons, through the hypocrisy of men that speak lies, branded in their own conscience as with a hot iron."

This is from the RSV. Instead of "branded" the King James says "seared." A more freewheeling version, the CEV says,

"Their consciences have lost all feeling."

This is not a translation, but it does explain, in this case, the true meaning.

Beware of the conscience that has lost all feeling! We do it to ourselves when we continually reject the teachings of God's Word. It can happen to the alien sinner who reaches a point where the word does not have power to move him to repentance because he has cast it aside so many times that his conscience gives up.

It happens also to the Christian when he begins to drift away from a close walk with God and begins to say, "I know I should but ..." Like the sense of smell and other senses, there comes a time when the function has been so often assailed that it says, "I'm not being listened to so why continue to send the message!"

Praise God if your conscience still works! Nurse it back to health if it doesn't. It may be a blessing if your nose shuts out a disagreeable odor. But if your conscience shuts out the word of God, the power of salvation is inaccessible!

Doyle Goodspeed

WHAT THE CROSS SAYS

ON THE SHOULDER OF THE ROAD, THERE appeared a styrofoam cross. As I came nearer, I could see the lettering, "MARCUS." The cross was decorated simply. Only that. A cross. A name. A little decoration. But it spoke volumes. It says there was a crash on the highway. At least one man or boy was killed. He was loved by someone. He is missed by someone. There are tears that are being shed. There is a home with great sadness. Lives have an empty place. That is what that cross said.

There were other things the cross itself did not say. Who was Marcus? Where did he live? Where was he going when the accident took his life? Who are the ones who loved him so much they went to the trouble of erecting the cross? What are the empty places that will remain unfilled? What kind of life had he lived?

There was another cross. Like parentheses, two others stood, one on either side. But the one in the middle is the one with the message. It tells of an execution. It speaks of indescribable suffering. It attests to blood shed. All things have some reason. What was the reason for this cross?

Centuries before this cross was lifted into its socket, the prophet had answered these questions. The prophet said,

> "All we like sheep have gone astray, we have turned every one to his own way; and the Lord laid on him the iniquity of us all." (Isaiah 53:6)

The penalty assessed the one on this cross was for our sins. What had he done to deserve such a terrible death? Nothing. What did we do? Countless things for which we could never atone. In the same chapter, the prophet had said, "He was wounded for our transgressions, he was bruised for our iniquities: the chastisement of our peace was upon him; and with his stripes we are healed."

The cross says that someone loved me enough to step forward and say, "I will accept the penalty for his errors, I will pay for his mistakes."

The penalty which I deserve is eternal death or separation from God.

> "The wages of sin is death; but the gift of God is eternal life in Jesus Christ our Lord." (Romans 6:23)

It is incredible that someone would love me enough to bare his back to receive the lashes which were my due. But that is what the cross insists is true.

The cross shouts victory! Sadly, there will come a time when my name, or yours, will be on the styrofoam cross, or in the obituaries and on the sympathy cards the family will receive from concerned friends.

Were it not for the cross, that would be an appropriate time for dejection and dread. Instead, it can be a celebration of joy because,

> "The sting of death is sin and the strength of sin is the law. But thanks be to God who gives us the victory through our Lord Jesus Christ." (I Corinthians 15:56-57)

Our victory is through Christ and His victory is through the cross. That's what the cross says.

Doyle Goodspeed

REVERENCE AND THE NEW WAVE

THERE IS A VAST CHASM BETWEEN THE trivial attitude found in the present day toward divinity and the attitude of the ancient Jews. Those Jews held the name of Jehovah in such reverence they would not even speak it lest they be guilty of using it in vain. In a news magazine article emphasizing the spread of a certain type of religious thought, the headline read, "Yo, Where's My Bible?" It was stated that, among celebrities, the favorite T-shirt was one with a picture that was supposed to be of Christ. Beneath it, in large letters, it says, "JESUS IS MY HOMEBOY." While it is good that interest in Christ and God may be escalating, the trivializing of the Creator of the Universe and His only begotten Son is not.

The Holy Spirit highlighted the reverence of Nehemiah for our example. Notice how he referred to God as he prayed.

> "I beseech thee, O Lord God of heaven, the great and terrible God, that keepeth covenant and mercy for them that love him and observe his commandments..." (Nehemiah 1:5)

Later, in the same book, in chapter 9, verses 5b-7, we have another example:

> "...blessed be thy glorious name, which is exalted above all blessing and praise. Thou, even thou, art Lord alone; thou

> *hast made heaven, the heaven of heavens, with all their host, the earth, and the things that are therein, the seas, and all that is therein, and thou preservest them all; and the host of heaven worship thee. Thou art the Lord the God, who didst choose Abram, and brought him forth out of Ur of the Chaldees, and gave him the name Abraham. "*

We cannot have the reverence that our God demands if we look upon Him as an equal. Looking at another example from the Old Testament, in the Book of Job, Job, a righteous man who had the approval of God but had been smitten with infirmity by Satan, is searching in his own mind for a reason for his plight. God rebukes him by saying,

> *"Who is this that darkeneth counsel by words without knowledge?" (Job 38:2)*

Job answers in chapter 40, verse 4,

> *"Behold, I am vile; what shall I answer thee? I will lay mine hand upon my mouth. "*

Job would never look upon God as his homeboy. God was one who deserved the utmost respect.

A lack of awe and respect and reverence for Almighty God will not lead to the obedience and service that is due Him. And it is impossible to pay the homage to God essential to true worship without an overpowering realization that His thoughts and His ways are as much higher than ours as the heavens are above the earth.

> *"For my thoughts are not your thoughts, neither are your ways my ways, saith the LORD.*
>
> *For as the heavens are higher than the earth, so are my*

ways higher than your ways, and my thoughts than your thoughts." (Isaiah 55:8-9)

While it is encouraging that more people are taking note of God, they need to realize that,

"Not every one that says unto me Lord, Lord, will enter the kingdom of heaven but he that doeth the will of my Father which is in heaven." (Matthew 7:21)

Jesus is not our "Homeboy." He is our Lord, and Master.

Doyle Goodspeed

FAITHFUL

CLEANING OUT THE ATTIC

WHEN WE BOUGHT THIS HOUSE, THERE was a mounded area in the back yard, beautifully grassed over, that intrigued us. We jokingly wondered if it might be a grave. Later we found that indeed it was a grave! The prior owner had a beloved dog she had buried there. When we smoothed the mound to put in a goldfish pond, we found that from "dust thou art and unto dust shalt thou return" was true of dogs, just as it is of humans. But that experience did not embolden us to look up in the attic. My brother looked in his attic and found that several years ago, the roofers that replaced a wood shingle roof with a composition one and had left most of the debris in his attic. He has spent several days carrying all this trash out and still has a long way to go. So I don't know whether it is better to worry about what might be up there or risk a peek. My imagination brings pictures of not only trash, but also all kinds of fearsome critters. So you can see the dilemma.

Of this one thing I am sure, in the attic of our minds, also a fearsome place, there are many housecleaning jobs that could be done. In I Corinthians 13:11 Paul said,

> *"When I became a man I put away childish things."*

No matter what the age, after a dedicated search within ourselves there are usually leftover attitudes and qualities from our childhood behavior that could be discarded. Petulance, sensitivity to slights and playing at religion can keep us from being what we want to be and what God wants us to be,

In Ephesians 4:25-32 Paul speaks of a general housecleaning that is of great benefit. He tells us to put away lying, anger and stealing in the first three verses. And continues to remind us to get rid of corrupt communication and speak those things that build up. He concludes by admonishing,

> *"Let all bitterness, and wrath, and anger, and clamor, and evil speaking and malice be put away."*

And then, on a positive note, tells us to be kind to one another, tenderhearted, and forgiving.

Many of our bad qualities go undetected (by us, not by others) because we hesitate to see what's in the attic, and yet scripture is filled with suggestions that self-examination is essential to living a life that will have the approval of God. Weekly, as we partake of the Lord's Supper, we are to,

> *"...let a man examine himself and so let him eat of this bread and drink of this cup." (I Corinthians 11:28)*

And in his second letter to the Corinthian church Paul said, "Examine yourselves whether ye be in the faith; prove your own selves." In some things, what you don't know can hurt you!

Doyle Goodspeed